Living with **Autism**

My Life With God, Me, and Melvin

Bernadette Butler

PAGE PUBLISHING, INC.
New York, NY

First originally published by Page Publishing, Inc. 2018

Cover art by Demetrious Reed

ISBN 978-1-64138-604-3 (Paperback)
ISBN 978-1-64138-605-0 (Digital)

Printed in the United States of America

Acknowledgments

First giving honor to the Father God—he is teaching me to see life in a loving way.

I would like to thank all of my friends who stuck by me through the years and helped me to help my son.

To my husband Paul who encouraged me to tell my story.

To all the mothers with autistic children and adult children, there is HOPE.

Introduction

I was a child that was set aside. No word of encouragement and not many dreams to fulfill. I was stagnant until Melvin came into my life.

I was nineteen, graduated from a business college, had a full-time job, and I was pregnant.

I was not going to have an abortion; somehow, I must find a way to have my baby and keep him.

I was insecure and fearful. I was afraid of my mother and what she would do. My mother is strong willed and overbearing. She would impose her will upon you, right or wrong. If you did not do as she said, she would tell you that nothing good will happen for you. God will punish you. To say I was afraid of her would put it mildly. I was terrified. I was concerned about what she would do to me. Her words could hurt just as the blow to my head. My mothers' love is complicated. I remember how she told my oldest sister to have an abortion. I decided to hide my pregnancy as long as I could. I would deal with the consequences later.

I remember when I first felt his movements. I was coming from work on the train. It felt like butterflies. I smiled.

I needed a doctor to confirm my pregnancy. The boyfriend took me to Planned Parenthood. I was examined. I never had a Pap test before, so I was unclear about what would happen.

I don't recall if the person was a nurse or a doctor. It was the fall 1974.

I was nervous. When I was called into the exam room, the standard procedure was to take off my clothes and put on a gown.

She came into the room, asked me questions, and then began the exam. At the end of the exam, she balled her fist and rammed it inside of me, my body shook like jello. She stated she need to see how many centimeters I was. I now believe this was not the concern. I was about six weeks. I believe she attempted to interrupt the pregnancy. One thing for sure, I was not going back to that place.

I left the building and told him what happened, including the first incident. He didn't care; he just wanted the confirmation of me having a baby.

I was pregnant—what to do? I did not tell my mother; she figured it out. I was married three months before delivery.

I wanted to believe it would all work out for the better.

The ideal life is a home with a white picket fence, two children perfect in every way. You envision your children growing up, going to college, getting a well-paying job, marrying and having at least two children.

These ideas always surface when you have your firstborn.

What happens when that is not the case? What do you do? What happens when your spouse points the finger and says it must have been something you have done, or your in-laws begin to whisper that the child is not his, or this came from her side of the family, or she slept with her stepfather, that is why? What do you do when your own family is silent? No words like, "Can I help?" or "Do you need someone to talk to?" or "I am here for you." What do you do when all fingers are pointing at you and accusing you by saying, "I know you"?

I Know You

I know you, they said
Yes, I know you
You don't know me was my reply
You don't know me, these are the reasons
Why.

Were you there when the tears fell

From my eyes?
Were you there when I was told the hope
I had for him could never be?
Were you there when the despair cast a
Shadow over me?
Were you there when I fell to the floor
In grief?
Were you there to comfort and give me some
Peace?
Were you there when he begun to talk to me
This is something I was told could
Never be?
Were you there when my heart burst with
Joy, like a shooting star
Flying across the sky?
Were you there when my hope for him began
To spring up within me?
Were you there when he spoke to me and
Began to direct the way?
Were you there when he turned my
Sorrow into joy?
Christ was there for me through
It all.
Christ was there before the teardrops
Began to fall.
Christ was there, I tell you,
Through it all.
Christ spoke words of encouragement
To me.
Believe when I say
Christ is the father of us all
Who knows me
He knows me.
He knew me when I was formed in my
Mother's womb.
He knows my every need.

He knows all of my sorrows
And all my heart's desire.
He knows the plans for Melvin
And me.
In him I trust
To him I call and depend.

Who knows me
He who created all things.

To say the least, this was going to be a great challenge for me. No support from either family, except for my aunt-in-law who lived in Northern California.

How do you begin to help when you don't know the way to go? This was a challenge to my faith in God. On this journey, Jesus Christ was teaching me his eternal promise. "I will never leave you, nor forsake you."

This is a story about the birth and life of my autistic son born in 1970s.

Christ was taking an opportunity to heal a brokenhearted young woman who grew up in a volatile, abusive home—to begin a healing journey and rewrite a new life's story.

This journey began with Melvin.

Chapter 1

I loved being pregnant. I had someone to distract me from the circumstances that were going on around me. I was desperate for someone to love me. Like a dry leaf that fell from a tree on a hot summer day. I was thirsting for recognition and I hungered for love. I now had someone to distract me from the circumstances that were going on around me.

I went to an OB doctor. He was my aunt's doctor. He agreed to take me. I was six months by then. I didn't show a tummy until I was seven months. I was nineteen going on twenty.

I went to a two-year business college in Chicago and got a job working at an office in downtown Chicago. The pay was good. I did not have medical insurance. I did not think to get it, not even for myself. He had a part-time job, nothing promising, until a friend of mine that I worked with told him to see her husband for a job. We lived with my mother and paid her rent.

The first pain I got, I did not know what was happening. I began to throw up. I called my husband at work and then my best friend. When we got to the hospital after the exam, they sent me home. I was not ready to deliver.

Later that afternoon, oh boy, was it time! When we got to the emergency room, they were wheeling me fast into a room. I was told by the nurse to change and put on the hospital gown. She walked out of the room and left me without extending a helping hand. I was in pain. As I rose out of the wheelchair, I noticed blood in the seat. I looked down and I was soaked in blood. My pants were bloody. I knew I would need to throw them away. Everything was a mess. I managed to put the hospital gown on but blood continued to flow. I was embarrassed and confused. I did not understand what was going on. I told the nurse when she returned to the room that I was bleeding. She did not respond.

I was hurting, of course; but again, this was my first child. I didn't know what to expect.

My doctor couldn't make it, so the doctor on call was the person to assist in the delivery.

He said, "You won't feel anything soon," and he put a mask over my nose." I was livid and my heart was pounding. Fear flooded my mind. I recalled the surgery I had at fourteen years old. I could have died then. Am I going to die now? That was the last thought I had.

I do not remember anything other than my name being yelled. Then I heard, "You have a son."

I said, "I was asleep, how do you have a baby asleep?"

The next day, my OB doctor said that Melvin was fine and healthy. The nurse brought Melvin to me. I thought I would burst. This was the person who moved around inside of me for nine months. He was beautiful.

In the back of my mind were still those lingering questions as to what happened to us during the delivery.

Later in my life, after giving birth two more times, I knew what happened to Melvin. The doctor pulled him out with those long tongs. That explained the marks he had on the side of his head.

My experience in the delivery room with Melvin kept me from accepting any meds during delivery with my other two children. It hurt, but I would rather have the pain than to have any more questions. I relied on Jesus.

I love Melvin so much. I knew the basics: feed, change the diaper, comfort, and bath. I sang to him. I played classical music for him. I had all those dreams and hopes for him.

My ideal family was always happy. My family life growing up was always in turmoil. I thought I could create this ideal loving family. That was not the case.

When Melvin cried at night or woke for a feed, I was told to get up and take care of him because that was my job as a woman. I did not disagree with that, but I thought that sometimes, we could do it together. Cuddle and love our baby and each other. Perhaps I just read too many fairy tales.

When Melvin was four months old, we moved to Southern California. I had never been away from my family members no matter how dysfunctional they were. *Dysfunctional* is a kind word for sin, a family living life without Jesus being the center. I wanted a family where Jesus was the center.

Here I am going to a state that I may have heard of and seen pictures of in a book or magazine. I never flew before, so my fears and anxiety was at an all-time high. I was holding my baby tight. I know that Melvin could feel the fear in me. When that plane took off into the sky, all sense of understanding escaped me.

The flight attendant could see it. A few of them tried to ease my fears. It didn't work. Every bump I thought was a death sentence. My concern was to protect my child the best I knew how. The husband ignored me the entire time. There was no sympathy for me.

When we began to land, I thought the takeoff was the worst experience ever; the landing process was beyond what I thought during the takeoff. Nonetheless, when the plane landed, I said I wasn't going to fly again. (I didn't know God's plan for me.)

I came outside the airport area with my baby in my arms, a new marriage, and in a new state.

I did not know God's plan for me.

It was Melvin, me, and his dad.

Chapter 2

We stayed with his brother in a two-bedroom apartment. He went to look for work in the day until the evening. It was just Melvin and me.

I kept the apartment clean, and I cooked. I wasn't the best cook at the time, but I knew the basics.

The marriage was turning sour, and it was not a year. I had a lot of emotional problems. I was on edge all the time. Growing up in a verbally abusive, volatile home took a toll on me. I was now an adult with a husband and a baby. What was I to do? The type of marriage I did not want was what I had. He was unkind, verbally and at times physically abusive and extremely demanding. It was his way or the highway. He would often say, "I am ninety-nine point nine percent correct." I come to realize I had married my mother.

I made a decision to go back to Chicago with my son and file for divorce.

I felt trapped. I was not in a good situation in California, but I knew deep in my heart that I would not be welcomed back at home, because my mother was angry when we told her we were moving to California. Before I left she said I was not loyal to the family and nothing good will happen. She was going to strike at me with Melvin in my arms. I was tried from the confrontation and I told her go ahead and hit me. Her arms were lifted high in the air and then she walked out of the room. We left that night and stayed with his sister until we left for California two days later. I had nowhere to go, so I stayed.

There is an old saying, "You made your bed, now lay in it." I laid in it and often suffered for it.

Melvin was not a fussy baby. He laughed and cooed. He was easy to take care of. I never thought at the time anything was out of the ordinary. When we attended church, Melvin cooperated as any other child. Sometimes, it was a long service. I had snacks for him, and often, he would take a nap. I did not know how to drive, so we rode to and from church with my brother-in-law.

As time passed, there were no telltale signs of anything out of the ordinary. Melvin did not like to crawl on the floor, so he learned how to walk before he was one year old. His eating habits were good. He was not a picky eater. He had all his vaccination shots in a timely manner. He potty-trained before two years old. At two and half years old, Melvin had not developed a speech pattern. He hummed and made ah sounds.

My initial thought was because we had no relatives his age in California, and we were isolated from other children, he needed to be given opportunities to interact with others, so I placed Melvin in the children's choir at church (the tiny tots).

I was trapped in fear. Afraid of my own shadow. The park was directly across from the apartment building where we lived. I was afraid to go across the street. I could not walk a block from the apartment. Melvin's world needed to expand beyond me and the apartment. This was not about me; this was about Melvin's life. I must step out of this fear.

I started walking with Melvin. We bought a stroller, and out we went, to the park, shopping, everywhere we could go without getting lost. This was good for me and good for Melvin.

To ensure Melvin could get into more activities, I needed to learn how to drive. I could not depend on my spouse to take us out anywhere. I tried to learn with him, but that was a total disaster; it always began and ended in a fight. He had no patience with me.

I was working as a temp at one of the universities in California. I asked a stranger to teach me how to drive. Taking drastic measures were needed.

The spouse did not care who taught me how to drive so long he did not have to. I was nervous, but after two weeks of lessons, I was ready to take my driving test. I FAILED the driving portion.

Of course, I had to wait for another attempt. The second time was a charm.

Melvin and I could get around more quickly. Now I can take him to his doctor's appointments without depending on someone else. We could go to church on our own and stay for other activities.

Melvin and I rode in a 1964 Chevy Malibu. The upholstery was torn, but I made covers for it. Melvin enjoyed riding in the car. He sat next to me. There were no seat belt laws during that time.

One morning, his aunt asked if I would give her a ride to work. On the way home, I saw a train coming. This train track had no light and arm signal. I stopped suddenly, and Melvin rolled out of the seat onto the car floor.

He looked at me as if to say, "Are you kidding me!"

He got up and went to the back seat. He did not ride in front with me until he was a teenager.

So you see, I did not think Melvin had a disability because he processed that his mother at the time was not a good driver, and to stay safe, he went to the back seat. He understood and acted upon without saying a word.

Chapter 3

When Melvin was three and half years old, he did not have words nor could he form a sentence verbally.

His form of communication was pointing. I had his hearing tested at the John Tracy Clinic. I thought Melvin was deaf, but the test results stated otherwise.

Now I am confused. What is going on? I made another appointment with his pediatrician. He said that Melvin's checkup was normal. He asked me not to worry about delayed speech; some children did not speak as quickly as others.

The doctor said, "He is an only child, think about getting him a dog for companionship." He also said, "When Melvin points at what he wants, let him say what he wants, do not just give it to him."

We did not get the pet, but when Melvin pointed at an apple, I would say, "Say apple."

He replied, "Apple."

He began saying single words, and I was happy for that. My hopes were high. Maybe he had delayed speech after all.

We often took afternoon naps. Melvin woke before I did. I felt him moving around. So I just lay there with my eyes closed hoping that I could get a little more rest.

The most extraordinary moment happened. Nothing I ever suspected. Melvin came close to me and said, "This is my mommy," and he kissed me on my cheek. My heart was leaping for joy. When I opened my eyes, he turned his head as if not a word was ever spoken.

This was my hope, to bring out the moment again. I waited for that. This very act motivated me to pursue the help for Melvin, and no one was going to stop me.

At four years old, I enrolled him into preschool. My thought was, if he was around more children to play with, this would help because Melvin was around me all the time. I bought him a backpack, and off he went two days a week.

The preschool building was built like a little castle. It was a program provided by the park system. I was so excited for Melvin, and I thought all the troubles would go away. Melvin would be normal. After three to four weeks, the preschool teacher told me that he did not interact with the children. He played by himself. She told me something was wrong, and I should have him checked for a disability.

I could not believe what I was hearing. I cried, and that is when I first heard the word *autism*.

I did not know anything about this word and what it meant. I went to the local library and asked for books on autism. I recall the clerk asking me why.

I told her, and she said, "How old are you?"

My guess was, she thought because of my age and my first child, how could he be autistic?

This is a complex disability at so many different levels. It is an unknown word; it is a title that they are attaching to my son's name.

I was devastated. I did not know how to help my son. I was in an unstable marriage at twenty-three, but I felt like I was fifty. I prayed so hard, asking God for the direction I needed to find help for my son.

We were referred to one doctor after another. It was draining and very tiring for both of us. I read every book I could find. I learned how to cook certain foods that would help. I went to the health food stores. I stayed away from food with dyes.

I cried, and I prayed and began to cry all over again. There was no one I could depend on, not even his dad.

After every tear that fell from my eyes, the determination within me grew even stronger than my sorrows.

I must have a plan. I must take action. Lord lead the way.

Chapter 4

First to tackle the eye contact. If he was not looking at me when I was speaking to him, how would he know what to do? I would make sure that he was looking at me. This was not an easy task because Melvin was hyperactive, and looking at me or anyone else in the eyes was upsetting to him.

In order for me to keep his attention for more than three minutes, I would give him what he liked.

Another way I reached him was having story time. He loved Winnie the Pooh stories with all Pooh friends. His favorite was Tigger and Piglet. I would imitate the voices of each character. He loved it, and this also encouraged him to repeat what I said. He would laugh, take his hands put it on my face and say Tigger, and I would make Tigger sounds. This was great.

I was feeling in the dark as to what would work and what would not work. I knew, for sure, if Melvin was upset, he would completely shut down. I tried to keep whatever we did fun and light and not extend beyond his attention span. It is like building blocks. If you rush in stacking the blocks, they will fall. If you take your time and be patient, you can stack the blocks as high as they can go.

Certain family members started telling others that Melvin was someone else's child. Other statements were made such as she made him retarded, and no one in our family has a child like him. I was told my son would be taken away from me because I was not doing the right things for him, and that's why he is like that.

Some of them would speak to Melvin as if he was unintelligent. Whenever they saw him, they would repeatedly say, "What is your name" throughout the entire visit.

Melvin would grow impatient each time he was around them and would become anguished and uncomfortable. It would take until once we were back home to settle him down. Can you imagine what he was thinking about this interaction with certain family members?

This lack of understanding was coming from both sides of the family. I was becoming a bitter person toward both sides, mine as well as my husband's.

Our life was going in and out of doctor's offices. Trying to find someone who could help me and not discourage me. By now, there were several different diagnoses.

I enrolled Melvin with an organization that helped us. We were sent to many different psychiatrists. I remember one who told me that Melvin would eventually be back in diapers. He stated that Melvin would never function as a normal person. He also told me never to have any more children because Melvin would harm the child.

Can you imagine, I was not twenty-five years old, and I was told not to have any more children because my son would harm the child! After the doctor told me this, I looked him in the eyes and said, "When you become God, then you can tell me something." I walked out that office more determined to find a way for my son to have a life of his own. When we returned home from that visit, I put Melvin to bed so he could rest.

As I washed the dishes preparing dinner, I talked to God. I would say to God, "Why me? What is going to happen to my son? He will never have a family. What did I do that you are angry with me?"

I thought about when I was a child. There was a little boy who lived next door to us. Every Saturday morning, he would get up, go outside, and swing back and forth. He did not talk, he just would swing. The noise of the swing would awaken me. I would get angry. When I went out to play later in the day, if he was outside, I would throw pebbles at him. Now I thought I was being punished for that.

Mistreating someone who had not harmed me in any way. This memory haunted me for a very long time. I said, "This is my crime."

I would cry, yell, and roll on the floor; but when I was finished, another idea would come to me. God was helping me, and I did not realize it at the time.

I found another program for autistic children at one of the universities. The parents were required to bring the child to the university once a month. The college students would come to your home and work with your child through a program that the doctor designed.

Melvin knew his colors; he could tell time, count, and add. I taught him these tasks with a program I developed with him. I felt the university program would help Melvin even more and assist me to further Melvin's progress.

At first, I thought the university program was helpful. Then Melvin was not cooperating anymore. The time that was spent was two hours twice a week. Melvin was told to sit in a chair. When he gave eye contact, the student would say, "Good boy," and give him a raisin.

The letter *A* was placed before him. He had to say it was an *A*. Melvin knew his *ABC*s, so when he was to repeat it many times, he would try to leave the chair. The student then would say, "Sit." If Melvin's hands left his lap, the student would say, "Hands down."

These sessions went on for more than a month. Melvin was tired of them, and so was I. I had read that doctor's book and his theory on why some children are autistic. One thing that I did not agree with for sure is, no one was going to use shock treatment of any kind on my son.

The last straw was when the students came and Melvin began to withdraw. Instead of them saying they will try tomorrow, they said, "We will give him a break today." They bore down harder on him, and he began to scream and cry.

I went into the room and told them to stop. Even I would get tired of someone telling me, "Hands down," and forcing me to eat raisins when I do not want any.

One student challenged me, and I told that person, "When you pay bills in my home, maybe you can have something to say." I told them to get out of my house.

When meeting at the university that month, I told the doctor, in front of the other parents, that I did not want the students at my home and I was taking Melvin out of the program. I also informed the parents to watch out for the use of electric shock on their children if they say and do the wrong command.

My only hope was to enroll Melvin into a public school system and hope they would work with me.

Oh boy, here we go.

Chapter 5

At the age of five years old, I sent Melvin off to school. I was excited and afraid at the same time. I did not know what would happen, but I was determined that my son would receive an education and not be set aside somewhere.

Melvin accepted the fact that he was somewhere else during the day other than home. Kindergarten was a challenge! The teacher suggested that Melvin attend the school for the mentally disabled, and I insisted that he stay put.

The staff and the principal did not want to deal with Melvin because of me. They felt I was pushy.

The school bus would pick Melvin up, and he would be dropped off at school. One day after Melvin left for school, I felt the need to make sure he got there safely. When I called the school secretary in the principal's office, I was told he did not come today. My reply was, "I know that I sent him. Find my son!"

I immediately got in the car and went to the school. A neighbor that lived across from the school saw him wandering around in the neighborhood park. The neighbor took him to the school. I was extremely upset! I brought Melvin to school each day and picked him up.

I now understand the school's concern. There were very few programs for autistic children, if any. Melvin was going to school. I am a taxpayer.

When first grade came around the principal and staff, including Melvin's new teacher started documenting my son so they could remove him from the classroom. The teacher stated it was hard to work with him.

An IEP meeting was set up. This was the first time that I had ever heard the term IEP (Individualized Educational Program). It included the teacher, principal, and other staff members at the school.

Parents who go with no representation sometimes do not understand the educational jargon that is used.

I called for help. The organization Melvin was enrolled in had people who could attend the IEP meeting with me. They helped me address the need of my son.

Since the school was documenting Melvin, I started documenting the school.

I would drop Melvin off, park my car somewhere out of sight and go back to peek into the classroom. I saw the teacher treating my son differently than she would the other students in the classroom.

Each day, I would drop him off. That was the routine of the day until one day, the principal was waiting for me and escorted me into her office.

I was told I could not peek into the classroom. I was disturbing the teacher. I informed her I was not comfortable with how my son was being treated. I was told that Melvin was not capable of doing the work. He did not know his colors, shapes, animals, ABC's, and how to tell time.

I was stunned by what I heard, but I knew that he could say and do all that she said he could not.

Construction paper was put on the window to keep me from peeking in, so I decided to go into the classroom. Each morning, I signed in at the principal's office, put a badge on and went into the classroom.

To my surprise, Melvin was not answering the questions correctly. When Melvin saw me, he sat up in his seat and began to answer the teacher correctly. He did everything she pointed at on the board. I told Melvin when we got home we are going to have a little talk.

I explained to him when the teacher asks him a question and he knows the answer, he should say the answer; but if he does not know, he should say, "I do not know."

Did Melvin truly know what I was explaining to him, probably not because it took a while for his brain to process what was being said to him, let alone trying to respond back. I would speak to him like I would another child. I tried not to treat him different.

I came to learn if Melvin felt that you expected him to say or do something stupid or treated him like he was, he would respond to you like he did his teacher. If you expected nothing from him, Melvin gave you nothing. If he felt that you really cared about him, then he would respond in a positive manner. He would let you in.

I was pregnant with my second child. In the back of my mind, I recalled what the doctor had told me. Melvin was going to hurt the baby if I had another. The doctor gave no medical reasoning for this. Nothing to back up such a strong statement. He said it as a matter of fact. I was determined to prove him wrong.

I explained to Melvin that I was having a baby. When I began to show, I let him touch and say hello to the baby. When the baby kicked, he would feel it and begin to laugh. I had no more fear of Melvin harming his soon-to-be baby sister.

When our daughter was born, he was excited. He would help me by getting the items I needed, such as diapers, lotion, etc. He watched her every move. He was very protective of her. He played with her, and he showed her how to wink her eye. I took a picture of that.

Just as Melvin was protective of her, she was protective of him. She would instinctively watch for him.

I taught Melvin how to ride a bike. If he strayed too far, his sister would call out and say, "Mailman, come back here, Mailman." That is how she pronounced his name.

He is five years older than her and ten years older than his youngest sister. He has never harmed them. They had their moments with each other. For example, he would not let them in his room because he said they were messy. Melvin's room was immaculate. Once I thought it was him messing up the bathroom. He told me, "That's those girls who mess up the bathroom."

Everyone had their chores including Melvin.

When I had more children, this taught me to stop smothering him so much. I had to learn to allow him to grow independent of me.

When I was in high school, a student who we called the black Tony Curtis had Down syndrome. How brave were those parents to send their child to a public school setting. Guess what, Tony received most popular when we graduated. Yes, Tony walked when the class of 1972 walked. The principal at the school did not remove Tony, the teachers worked with him.

At the time, there were no public school special education budgets. There were no designated special education programs. I wanted Melvin to have that same opportunity. I cannot speak for Tony's parents, but just maybe, they thought he is living in this world, and he had to learn how to cope and live in it. To Tony's parents, I say, thank you.

The IEP meeting came, and I was unable to go. Therefore, his dad went in my stead. I had him to take all the tapes that I recorded at home with Melvin all the sessions that we had each day. I recorded Melvin reading, and those tapes were included.

I later found out that the teacher did not teach Melvin to read or sound out letters. Somehow, he remembered words. He could read the Matt's Mitt books. Did he understand at the time what he was reading? Could he express to me what he read? No, but I knew it was there; he just did not know how to get it out verbally.

There was a long debate his dad said at the meeting. They thought that I influenced Melvin into answering the questions. After listening to the tapes several times, the group came to the conclusion he was capable and did respond properly. Melvin was placed into a private school setting, and the public school paid for it.

The school was located in one of the beach areas in California. Melvin began to grow there. His teacher was amazing. She taught him sign language to help him communicate much easier. This tool was used until she was able to increase Melvin's vocabulary skills.

At that time, Melvin was on Ritalin. The teacher noticed that he started to behave differently. His doctor at the time wanted him to take a half a pill a day. The teacher said it made him like a zombie. I made the decision not give Melvin the pill anymore.

Melvin's time at the school was productive. They allowed me to volunteer my time in the classroom. Melvin was included in the Christmas program. I was happy but a little nervous about the outcome. Will he be able to sing in a larger setting? How would he react with an audience?

Melvin was excited about the program. That night, his little sister and I attended. We were the only black family! The program went well, and Melvin said his part. When the students began to exit the stage, my son refused to leave. He went to the podium and pretended to be the associate pastor at our church.

The associate pastor was seventy-five years old, and he trembled at times. Melvin began to imitate the pastor, his body language, the shaking of his hands, and mimicked his voice.

His sister said, "What is Mailman doing?"

I could have gone through the floor. Everyone was laughing, and I was embarrassed. The teacher finally was able to get Melvin to leave the stage.

Someone in the audience asked, "Whose child is that?" and the people looked at me.

Why not—I was the only black woman there.

When we got to the car, I asked Melvin, "Why did you do that?"

I was upset. He just looked at me. I calmed down and talked to my best friend about what happened. She began to laugh and so did I. I finally saw the humor in it. Melvin took his chance to shine, and shine he did. I still think about that day and chuckle.

I was holding on to Melvin, and in his way, he was saying, "Let me fly."

Melvin's teacher became a good friend of mine. She would stop by our apartment to check on Melvin's progress. I had someone to share my ideas about how to reach him. Her husband opened his heart and welcomed Melvin and me into their home. She didn't have to extend beyond the classroom, but she did. God blessed me with many people in my life who gave to me an extended hand of help as well as their friendship.

Chapter 6

We purchased a home, but it was not in the Los Angeles area. The home was sixty-five miles outside of LA. I was not familiar with their school system, but my assumption was that the school district would work with me. I was not correct in that thought! This was the next challenge. Now I was faced with my inner fears.

I enrolled Melvin into the school district. It was a small community at the time. Building of new affordable homes brought young families to the outline area. This new construction brought diversity into the community. Not just racially, but also families that had children with disabilities. This was a change that not only the city but the school district struggled with.

First on the list was finding a good pediatric doctor for my children. The hospital I took them to also had a doctor who specialized in disabled children.

Melvin's doctor was very encouraging. He listened and gave ideas on how to reach him and to help Melvin maintain the steps he had already accomplished. He enrolled Melvin into a sensory integration program at the hospital, a program developed for children with autism. The program helped Melvin on many levels. The mountain to climb was the school district.

On Melvin's first day of school in his new setting, I knew there would be some challenges which included Melvin's transition into a new environment. The small hurdle that I had in the LA district was nothing compared to the situation in this district. It was oil and water!

They had no programs that provided services for children with autism. The school district had Melvin evaluated numerous times.

They had put him into a special education classroom setting with fifteen students, one teacher and a teacher's aide. In the classroom were a variety of disabilities ranging from physical, mental, Down syndrome, and autism. There were many levels of disabilities. There were children who would self-inflict pain such as biting themselves and headbanging.

How was one teacher and one aide to handle the dynamics of this situation? It was not easy. I volunteered many times in the classroom with Melvin.

The IEP meeting was always a struggle because the school psychologist was busy telling me what Melvin could not do, and I was busy telling him what he could do and what he will be able to accomplish. Apparently, they wanted me out of the way. No one wanted to have anything to do with my son and me, but we were a package deal.

One day, the bus came to get Melvin and took him to school, but they did not tell me that my son was removed and sent to an entirely new school district outside of the county where we lived. The classroom was held in a trailer away from the school building. The students that attended that class were children who had behavioral problems and had been incarcerated with ankle bracelets on.

Reading this story, you, the reader, have an idea what my reaction would be. If you have that connection, you know I was on fire from head to toe. I called the superintendent's office and told them to get my baby out of that classroom. I was told that an IEP meeting must be arranged with the agreement of the team.

I did not send Melvin back to that classroom setting. I was told that I would be reported to the authorities. My response was to start dialing. They would have to put me in front of a firing squad before I allowed my son to step through those doors again. They would have to kill me first.

In the IEP meeting, of course the principal, teacher and the school psychologist stated that is where Melvin should be placed. I challenged it by calling for a hearing.

The hearing went in the favor of Melvin returning to the school district where we lived at. I did not have an advocate at the time. I had to learn quickly about speaking up for the needs of my son. This also included making phone calls to the State Board of Education, reporting out of compliance issues in the school district. I learned what my rights were as a parent and what my son's rights were. Melvin had two regular classes, and the remaining classes were special ed. This was a far cry from where they intended for my son to be. This was a battlefield, and I learned that I was not the only parent trying to get an adequate education for children that have special needs.

I wrote many letters including a letter to a public federal elected official. I saw his wife on a program speaking on children with disabilities. I was not expecting a reply, but I got one. The letter was sent to the Office of Civil Rights Education Division in Washington, D.C. from there to the San Francisco Division Office of Civil Rights. The division called the school district. Let's say I didn't have much resistance from the School District Office.

Most of the resistance came from a selected few teachers and the school board members at the time. I was once told at a school board meeting that my son would never be anything. The board and the superintendent felt that I was hostile, overbearing, and not willing to face the facts that my child would not be able to accomplish anything academically at all.

I would share my challenges with Melvin's pediatrician. He would laugh, but at the same time encourage me to continue the fight.

I started to receive phone calls from other parents asking if I would attend their child's IEP meetings.

The phone calls increased from parents with disabled children. I could not figure out how they were receiving my name and telephone number.

I never charged anyone when I attended IEP meetings with them. God had blessed me with so many helping me with my son. It was freely given and freely returned.

Later, I found out it was the pediatrician giving out my name. I laughed with him about that. He did not realize what a wonderful thing he did for me in sending me on a journey of freedom from my fears.

My journey expanded more than I ever could imagine for myself and Melvin.

Chapter 7

Attending many IEP meetings, I observed that parents who are nervous accepted whatever the teacher and the school psychologist decided for their child. Some parents would leave the meetings frustrated because they did not want the teacher to get upset if they did not go along with the suggested program. I would explain to the parents that the IEP meetings were a joint effort and that it is always good to include their ideas. They knew more about their child than anyone else. It could be the case that the child is willing to do more at home. The challenge is to carry that trust and willingness to the school setting. That is why the parents' input is extremely important.

I was not well received at the IEP by some of the teachers and principals. As my name was passed along in the community by parents of disabled children, my regular job became going to IEP meetings.

I met wonderful retired teachers who gave their time and tutored Melvin. He had some very dedicated teachers who were concerned about all students' outcomes. But there were some who had the belief that Melvin could not accomplish much of anything. This of course is a harsh reality of life for some of us with children with disabilities. We would like to think all teachers come with the hope and optimism that all children can learn, but they are human, and they bring in their personal beliefs into the classroom.

The school district, Board of Education, and the superintendent were not happy about me helping the parents and my volunteering at my children's school site. My struggles with the school administration and with some of my son's teachers was a backlash to my younger children. Some of their teachers at times viewed me hostile without any merit. Most teachers became uncomfortable because I was viewed as a community activist. This view of me extended from attending IEP meetings with parents. I will admit, when it came to the education of my children and others, I was passionate. I did not come to attack anyone but to defend the right of a fair, inclusive educational system for the disabled and disadvantaged.

A heavy banner to bare, but at the time, it was new, uncharted waters for children with autism. No one understood it! It was a testing ground for the educational and medical world as well as the parents who had children with this unfamiliar disability.

We lived in the desert area of California, in the summer; the heat rose above hundred degrees. One day I was volunteering, and I asked that the children not go outside because it was too hot. The response did not go over well. I was not the only parent who asked for the children to stay inside, but because of who I was, it was reported to the District Office.

I attended a school board meeting and asked the board to change the policy to allow the students to stay indoors or at least give the option of remaining in the cafeteria. The water fountains needed to work if the children chose to go outside. The principal at the site stated that I was always making trouble. The solution was to prevent me from coming on the campus, which also included picking up my children after school on a corner and not allowing me to step foot on school grounds. The board also used this rule to prevent me from assisting parents in IEP meetings. The battle lines were drawn!

I reported this in writing to the State Board of Education and to the Office of Civil Rights, the Justice Department Division. Other people in the community directed me to a parent organization from the Los Angeles area. Now I did it! I was in for a ride, and so was the District Office. I recall Betty Davis's line in a movie, *All About Eve*, "Hold on to your seat, it's going to be a bumpy ride." This was an understatement.

My friends and I went into prayer. In the meantime, I was approached by members of the community to run for the school board. I went into private prayer because if anyone was going to make that possible, it was Jesus. Whatever his will was for me, it will be so. Thus the journey that I was on with Melvin expanded even more beyond what I could have imagine.

I was summoned to a meeting in the principal office to receive the rules for picking up my child from school. My other daughter was in middle school, and the female principal there stated she had no problem with me and how I always worked and supported that school site. She did not prohibit me from picking up or volunteering on that campus, also the high school Melvin attended did not prevent me from picking up or volunteering.

Were some of the teachers pleased with me? No, they were not. Not because I disrespected them but because I challenged them in saying that my son was capable if given a chance. It was the elementary principal and a few of the teachers at that school who did not want me on school grounds.

The attendees of the meeting in the principal's office were the District Office representative and the school secretary. The night before, my friend and I had our own plan of action. We stated we will go in but not take a seat. We will pray and sing, "I am on the battlefield for my Lord." We would also read Psalm 35. We accomplished our mission, and they, of course, were in shock and speechless. They soon found their voice and gave me the rules.

I knew the representative from the school district because we were both involved in the community.

After he read the rules from the school board, I looked at him and said, "Now that you have sold your soul to the devil, where in the hell do you think you are going?"

Now, he was a tall, thin man, approximately six feet five. He was sitting in the chair, leaning back not too far but just enough to call himself intimidating. When I said this to him, he sat up straight. He had a certain look on his face, and the next thing we all witnessed him falling to the floor, chair, and all backward. I said to him, "You know you are wrong for this."

The district had security remove us from the office and escorted us off school property. As I was walking, I turned around and said, "This is not 1950 Alabama."

I was angry. I needed to direct that anger in another way. Parents began to petition for me to come to their children IEP meetings. Soon, the district could not prevent me from coming because the State Department of Education and the Office of Civil Rights did not support the district on how the matter was handled. I returned supporting the parents, but to pick up my younger daughter at the elementary school, the policy remained the same.

I did not know what to do. There is a story in the Bible that was placed on my heart. I told my friend, so I knew what I had to do. I did not want her involved because she was the only one who could take and bring my daughter to me from school. I was looking at fear in the face. Could I trust God and believe that the scriptures are true? So modern-day Joshua and Jericho was about to happen. The Lord had Joshua and the army march around Jericho for seven days and on the last day with a shout and horns. I was Joshua, and that elementary school was my Jericho.

Day one—I would say a prayer before I got out of my car and then walk. I walked around unnoticed by the principal. To most people, living in the houses around the school I was simply taking a daily walk. I would say a prayer when I was finished, get in my car and leave.

Day two and three were the same until day four. The principal came outside and stood and watched me for a while. He went back inside the school.

Fifth day: the principal came outside and began to yell at me, "Stop that!" He repeated several times. I ignored him and continued my walk. I realized that the entire school was aware of me doing this each day at the same time each day. Interesting, I thought the principal is aware of scriptures. On the sixth day of my walk, as I turned the corner, a man appeared and said to me, "Why are you walking? Why don't you walk half of the way instead of going all the way?"

I replied and said, "No, I will walk all the way." He repeated it again, and my reply was no different than the first time. He turned to leave and began to walk away, and I turned to see if he left. I saw him walk away, and then I did not see him at all. In this wide, open space, the school and the houses around. No door to a house or car closed. He was not walking down the street anywhere. I said to myself, "Humph!"

During this time, remember some of my friends approached me to run for school board. I agreed to do this but did not think about it much. I had no backing except from those who I knew. We had no money, just enough to have flyers made. One of my dear friends said, "Don't worry about that. We will knock on every door in the city and pass out our flyers. We will pray and trust God. Do not look at the circumstances; keep it moving. She passed out flyers on her job, other friends passed them out also. Parents were passing them out when they took their children trick or treating. I know because I was given one, when I was passing out candy!

The newspaper was doing a story on each candidate. Each candidate was backed by different organizations, realtors, teachers' union, and other wealthy, influential people. I, on the other hand, had prayers and fifty dollars! This was a shocker to the reporter. I know he was wondering how can she possible win a seat.

There were two seats. I was a new person to the community; I was not entrenched in the old politics of the town. This can be an advantage, and it can be a disadvantage. Money verses community is played out till this day.

To my surprise, I won the school board seat with the will of God, friends, flyers and fifty dollars.

The board and the superintendent were not happy. It was rumored the superintendent was rushed to the hospital that day.

I was not there to fight them. I was there to represent a voice that was silenced. Children with disabilities. I served two terms. That is another story.

Chapter 8

Getting what Melvin needed at school was an ongoing challenge. Some people continued to resist when it came to integrating Melvin into a regular classroom.

Melvin loved music of all kinds. He wanted to grow up to be a DJ; his favorite was Elvis Presley. I could not figure out where he heard any Elvis songs because I did not have any of his music. Melvin's second love was cars. He could tell you every car on the road. I bought him a model set to put it together because he asked for one. I asked him if he thought he could put it together, and he said yes. Well, Melvin showed me. He put that model car together without reading the instruction. The instructions were crumbled and put back in the box. I was overjoyed. I bought him three more.

When Melvin said he wanted to play an instrument, my answer was yes. Now, the band teacher was not enthusiastic about having Melvin in his classroom. I was not giving up. The music teacher could have strangled me. Other teachers sympathized with the band teacher. I would hear the chattering in the hallways of that high school, "He is not coming in my classroom, and I am not dealing with that crazy mother."

Melvin was finally included in the music classroom. Melvin could not pick up quickly how to play, but the fact he is exposed to something else was a victory in my eyes.

A door opened, he would not feel left out, he was included. Recall earlier in the story, I told you about a young boy whom we called Tony Curtis. We didn't exclude him. Everyone included him and made him feel that he was a part of the soon graduating class of 1972.

What happened to us? We had forgotten how to extend friendship, kindness, and love. I wanted what we had given Tony, I wanted that for my son; most importantly, Melvin wanted it for himself. He too had hopes, dreams, and visions for himself. God instilled in my son hope and dreams just like the rest of us. Because they do not all look alike, or they have a medical condition or disability does not mean that they do not have dreams and hopes of a better way for themselves. Instead, those of us who think we are perfect put road blocks in the way because we think they do not have the right to want more because in our eyes, they are not perfect. When I looked at my son, I saw the possibilities.

I had no intentions of taking Melvin out of that music class. I did not care if he learned to play that horn or not. He loved being in there. Most of the kids were not kind, but there were a few who would speak to him.

One day in class, as they were tuning up their instruments to begin to play, Melvin told one of the horn players that it needed tuning. At first, the teacher felt that Melvin was being a problem, but the teacher asked the student to play and the horn, indeed, needed tuning. The teacher could not hear this, but Melvin did.

When I picked Melvin up, the teacher said, "Did you know that Melvin has an ear?" and he proceeded to tell me the story.

He was excited. The teacher told me this is a gift. The teacher was beaming. Melvin became the person who the students had to warm up with before practice, and if the instruments needed tuning, Melvin assisted them. Later, the teacher said he was glad that Melvin was in his classroom and sorry that he gave me such a hard time. The band teacher was very nice young man once the smoke cleared.

Melvin had a teacher who was very supportive of him, and we became friends. If Melvin did not do the assignment, she would call; and when Melvin was not having a very good day emotionally, she would call me.

Melvin is very tall, and the football coach always tried to talk Melvin into playing football or basketball. The coach was also

Melvin's English teacher. He enjoyed Melvin in his classroom, and he often looked out for him during lunch time. I thank God for those teachers in Melvin's life who gave him a chance to try.

Melvin was also like other kids in high school, wanting to hang out and have friends. When he first started high school, it was not easy for him. Most kids were either making fun of him or afraid of him, or they tried to hurt him. In the second year of high school, things started to change for him. Some of the kids began to show a little more compassion.

In one of his classrooms, we had a situation. There was a girl that Melvin liked. She knew it and attempted to use it to her advantage. She started to get Melvin worked up (if you know what I mean), and it was getting to the point that he would not pay attention in class.

His teacher called me, and when I walked in the classroom, Melvin said, "All right, all right, I will do my work."

After class, Melvin and I went into the hallway. I proceeded to tell him about the reason why he was in school.

"You are there to learn," I reminded him, and if I had to come to school to be with him each day, I would. I am five feet three, and Melvin is six feet four. I came to Melvin waist area. Now this was after Betty Boo (that is what I called her, after she had Melvin worked up). I had to look up at Melvin because of his height, and I leveled my eyes and said to myself, *Oh no!*

After class, I talked with the teacher to come up with a plan of action. Betty would have taken my son to a place that even I could not bring him back once he'd been exposed.

Melvin began to tell me what Betty would say, "Melvin, had you ever had sex? Can I teach you something?"

Melvin said, "That is what she told me, Mommy. She told me I should listen to her."

Now this is clear that Betty tried to take advantage of my son's innocence.

I told Melvin, "You tell her the only person you are going to listen to is your mother. You do not need any instruction on sex at this present time, and the only new information you will learn comes from the book in the classroom."

Some children with disabilities are honest and will tell you everything, including informing you on what their response is. He told her, and let's just say she did not like the answer. She was sent to another classroom.

Melvin did have his share of girls that befriended him. One day, one of his teachers went into the lunch room and saw Melvin surrounded by several girls. One was rubbing his head; the other was making him laugh. Melvin was enjoying himself.

The teacher broke it up, and Melvin stated, "I was not doing anything with a laugh."

People's perception of children with any form of disability, they think they are less than human, as if they have no feelings. Some children with disabilities are isolated and not included. Although this type of thinking seems to be changing since Melvin's journey started, we still have a long way to go! Melvin and other disabled children are just like everyone else wanting to be accepted and understood.

Melvin's home life was challenging. His dad could not find a way to accept Melvin. He could not see the possibilities in him. His dad shot down the hopes and desires Melvin had for himself. His dad and I were often in verbal and sometimes physical fights about him. I did not like the things he said about our son. His dad wanted everything perfect, but nothing and nobody is perfect no matter how much we think we are.

There were a lot of other issues in our marriage that had nothing to do with the children; eventually, we had this huge fight, and I threw his clothes and him out.

There was calmness in the house. I was fearful about what would happen because I had no job, and how could I work with Melvin and his sisters needing me? Adding to these concerns, Melvin decided to test his wings.

For two years of high school, the bus picked Melvin up in front of the house, took him to school, and brought him back each day. One day, when the girls and I were outside cleaning up the front yard, his sister noticed that the bus had not come. So we went into the house, and I called the dispatch to find out why he was not home.

She called me back and said they will find out if he got on the wrong bus. We went back outside waiting for Melvin.

Then his sister said, "Look, Mama, there is Melvin."

My son had walked home from school. He crossed the streets and made it home safely. I nearly died. I was happy, but the fear of him and the danger that could have happened engulfed me. When you believe in God, you are not to be afraid.

All I could say to him was, "Well." I took a deep breath.

Melvin said, "I walked home, and I do not want to ride the bus anymore. I want you to drop me off at school and pick me up." He also said, "Do not let Dad come back."

I did let him come back because of my own fears of being with three children and one of them disabled. I did exactly what my mother did when she was married the second time to a violent man. I allowed my fear to overcome me instead of the peace that was in the home when their dad was not there.

The children's father had a lot of issues going on within himself. He wanted Melvin to become a reflection of him. Seeing this was not going to happen Melvin became for a lack of better words damaged goods. His dad often had him compete in basketball games with his cousins knowing that Melvin did not want to play. Melvin was ridiculed not only by his dad but by his uncle and cousins who did not see Melvin as a child of God. As Melvin became older, he started to resist. This did not sit well with his dad. It caused more conflict not only with Melvin but everyone.

You may ask what did you do? As I watched my in-laws' intolerant behavior toward my son, I am ashamed that I did nothing. I allowed his dad to control me as well as the children. I had no say so in the matter (so I thought). As Melvin suffered, I suffered with him. I kept quiet in front of them to keep the appearance—this image he was creating of the perfect family unit. When we would return home, that was when the verbal and sometimes violent acts occurred.

All I had to ask was, "Why did you do that to him?"

The arguments began and sometimes physical confrontation. I was boiling inside, and I knew that Melvin was too. This wonderful, loving child was beginning to fill with anger because his dad did not accept him, and at that time, his mother would not speak up for him. I knew that all this must change! I fought for Melvin at school; I must fight for him and the two girls at home.

Every Christmas holiday, the kids and I would decorate the house. I would cook the sweets that each one wanted. During the night, cookies were put in the plate for Santa; and in the morning, Melvin was the first to get up. The girls and I followed. We would open presents and later enjoyed our Christmas dinner.

Melvin loved the holidays, and when New Year Eve came, I would go to the store, buy the snacks each of us liked. I brought all kinds of party favors, plastic champagne glasses and bought apple cider, and that is how we toasted each New Year. Their dad was not a part of this. He would close the door and go to bed early. We would stay up and ring in the New Year. We played games all night until we fell asleep. It was during one of these celebrations that changed Melvin for good. We were downstairs, and right before midnight, he called Melvin.

"Melvin, you do not want to do that, come upstairs and come to bed."

I said, "Melvin, you do not have to go upstairs to bed you can stay."

"I know," he said, "but my dad said to go to bed."

That was the end of my silence. What son do you know who do not seek the approval of their dad? Till this day, he seeks the approval of his dad, and his dad continues to ignore him.

On my knees, I went to the Father in heaven and asked him for forgiveness for putting their dad and his immediate family before him (God). I would not let them in my home anymore with all their drama and turmoil that followed them wherever they went.

I stopped going with their dad to his family gatherings. Melvin told his dad he did not want to go because they do not like me. Of course, his dad accused me of putting that in Melvin's head. Melvin and I did not go, and soon, my daughters followed suit. I told their dad he could see his family all he wants, but they could no longer come to my home.

I had to face myself and all the fears that took hold of me. God put Melvin in my life to make me face those demons that were inside me and those dark clouds of despair that were with me since childhood. In order for me to protect Melvin, I had to protect myself. I prayed all the time. The Lord never left me even with my foolish thinking at times. He was instilling in me a will to go on. God was helping me face my fears, not all at once, but one bit at a time. A journey is a marathon, not a sprint.

Chapter 9

Letting Go

How do you let your children go when they have challenges? I wrestled with this all the time. In my mind, Melvin would always be with me. At times, even I shortchanged Melvin about his own personal feelings of himself. I wanted to protect him from family members and the world. I ached in my heart if anything ever happened to me who would see about my son. What would become of him, being at the mercy of the system in which we have allowed those who we vote for to have no compassion in their hearts for those who they feel are imperfect. I knew the time was nearing, Melvin would be a senior in high school. These thoughts nagged at me, I was always on edge. Not just because of what was personally happening in the marriage, staying involved in school with the other two children, being an elected official under scrutiny (especially if you are not what the good old boys had in mind). I was weighed down with the guilt that I carried for years about why did this happen to my firstborn child, I was a mess. I did not need anyone to beat me up because I beat myself up daily.

Melvin's senior year was upon us. They spoke about him receiving a certificate instead of a diploma. I wanted Melvin to have the opportunity to take the state test and get a high school diploma. I had resistance from one of his special education teacher. The math teacher's opinion was that he could not accomplish this. She did not support the idea at all. His primary teacher supported both Melvin and me and helped to prepare Melvin for the test. At an IEP meeting, I requested that Melvin have a modification to the test. This was offered to handicap students by law. The catch was you must be aware of your rights as a parent, so you can advocate for your child. Most parents at the time did not know. I informed as many parents I came in contact with. With a certificate, it would be challenging for a special-need student, at the time, to attend a two-year college setting. Again, at the time, it was sad that courses were not geared toward the strength of a disabled adult at a two-year college. The disabled adult would be in a better financial situation if they could manage themselves without assistance. I am pleased that times are changing. This was the transition period that occurs when the disabled student is about to leave high school. Depending on the disability, they can receive SSI. In my opinion, this assistance from the government without additional options can place the disabled adult on the poverty level and possibly one step from being homeless.

I was aware of Melvin's strengths and weaknesses. My hope and goal was to get him into a community college, but the support was not there for him at home by his dad. He discouraged Melvin for wanting to try.

When spring came, Melvin took the test. When the results came back, his primary teacher was jumping for joy. Melvin passed, and the teacher who was not supportive of Melvin told me that she learned a great lesson, not to give up on any of the kids! She thanked me! I do not remember her name. Maybe because she was one of the most negative of all the teachers. She was once his elementary teacher, and we were like oil and water. She did not want me around her classroom. So for her to tell me that was hopeful. It gave her a whole new outlook. I am not just happy for her but think of all the students that she had and was going to teach with a renewed hope. We give up so easily on those we feel do not measure up to our standards. When in fact we ourselves who think we are perfect do not measure up. We are simply a legend in our own minds. There is nothing wrong with anyone thinking positive about themselves, but when their thinking about themselves becomes a measuring stick toward others, that is where the problem lies.

I was proud as I could be at the graduation. Not only did I give the graduation speech on behalf of the school district, and I signed my son's high school diploma as vice president of the school board. As my son's name was called, he walked across the stage, and I shook his hand. I had to hold back my tears of joy. I would have flood the place out! All my friends who supported Melvin and me over the years were in attendance.

Later that evening, I thought about all the things that were said about Melvin by the professional doctors. I can hear the doctor that told me never to have any more children. Melvin got along with his sisters. It was what it should be. He did not allow them in his room because he did not want them touching his things. They had a typical brother-and-sister relationship. They understood their brother, and it never bothered them. If anyone said anything negative, they were quick to put them in their place. They defended their brother, and they love him.

The school board members were not happy about the good relationship that I was able to establish with the community. So like typical part line politician, they began to stir up the community against me, and they also attacked my children. One of Melvin's sisters spoke at a school board meeting about the comments that were printed in the local newspaper. I was proud of her. That put an end to the comments about Melvin. The other attacks continued. I eventually took the youngest daughter out of the school district and sent her elsewhere because of the vicious attacks and not just by parents but also by teachers who were strongly against me. Those teachers will never forget how I fought for my son. Most teachers supported me, and the rest did not want me there. Those are the ones who do not want parents involved because of the unknown to them. Some people, I think, are afraid to be challenged. And others feel you are attacking them personally when you ask questions or make suggestions; they feel you are confronting their knowledge. Remember, we are humans that operate from feelings instead of facts, or seeking what is true. We push away the things that we do not know, things that instill fear in us. Then we attack the very person that we fear.

Chapter 10

Melvin graduated, and the feeling of being disconnected set in. He was in a routine of going to school since the age of three. I was in the routine of taking my son to school and the other activities that Melvin was a part of. One activity he participated in was Boy Scouts. He earned a couple of patches. I knew the parents who did not mind Melvin being in the group. He was not into it, but he did like the Boy Scout uniform. The other activity that he participated in was karate on a military base near the city. My friend worked on the base, and her son was taking lessons. She talked to the instructor, and he gladly welcomed Melvin. He went twice a week. We had to get a pass to proceed on base, but I was so overjoyed that the instructor did not resist my friend's request. He encouraged Melvin and never gave up on him. He taught him that although you are challenged, you can achieve. Melvin earned a yellow belt. I was so proud of him. Soon, the base was closed to nonmilitary people, but I am thankful for the opportunity that they gave to my son.

What do you do when your routine has changed? Melvin did not know and neither did I. I wanted my son to stay with me, always to protect him from outside forces that were unkind to him. His relationship with his dad was declining rapidly. I do not know what his dad was thinking, but by his reactions, he seemed displeased that Melvin could not hold a job or attend college.

I mourned because I realized there would be no grandchildren for me from Melvin. Melvin would not experience fatherhood or dating for that matter, courting a young lady, going to movies, having lots of friends.

The environment at home was not the best, but it was still a cocoon, a bubble of shelter from the outside world.

The center helped to place Melvin in a work program. Melvin had a part-time job, making less than minimum wage.

The first job Melvin had was arranging hangers for a department store in the area. It appeared to go okay. He began to have problems in adjusting to a new setting. His case worker was helping him through the adjustment period. Then one day, I received a call from the warehouse saying that Melvin was bothering a worker. Melvin shared that a forty-five-year-old woman approached him, and she wanted to do things to him. I reported it to the center. After a second thought, I called the center back and stated that I wanted Melvin to go somewhere else to work. I would not take a risk of someone saying false allegations that could possibly land Melvin in jail. The center found another work program for him.

One of the many fears about Melvin was that he would be falsely accused and not be able to explain himself. This is not a far-fetched fear because young black males are always in question. Melvin's disability limited him in explaining himself; how could anyone who does not know him understand him? Melvin's physical body would have worked against him also. He is six feet four, and he could not explain himself to the police or anyone else. It would have been a nightmare if Melvin continued to work there. I was happy when the center found him another workplace.

As the tension between Melvin and his dad increased, I was at my wit's end. What should I do? I did not have a clear direction for Melvin or for me.

I was unclear, but Melvin was precise. Melvin had made up his mind. One day in the kitchen, he said to me, "Mom, I know something is wrong with me. My friends have gone off to college. I need my own place. I am a man."

My son was telling me "I am a MAN. It is time for me to fly. Let me go and sail this life." I knew I could not let him be totally on his own. There must be a way that he could experience it and yet have someone to watch over him.

I was unclear, but Melvin had just made my path clear. I called the center, and the search began for a placement. His dad did not object to this.

Trying to find a place for Melvin was a difficult task. Not because of Melvin but because of the sincerity of those who are caretakers of the disabled. It is a crime that we (society) do not demand that those in need are treated with respect and dignity. Some caretakers are in it purely for the money. Some, not all, do not care about the growth pattern of the young adults, and neither do those who make the laws that govern this area. Young adults who have different forms of disabilities should never be housed with young adults who have committed some type of crime, not because one is better than the other but simply because the need and care is different. My opinion is based on my experience during the time I was searching for a semi-independent living for Melvin. My hope is that this practice no longer exists.

I recall one home that we visited, and the lady who lived there had taken in at least four young men. When I first walked in, I did not like the upkeep of the home. My son grew up in a clean and orderly environment. When we sat down to speak with her and explain Melvin's needs, she quickly explained to me if Melvin was to strike at her, her boys would take care of him. I called the center and told them that home was not a fit home.

The next home we saw was a clean environment. The man appeared okay at the time. After several visits, we agreed that Melvin could stay there. I checked on Melvin often, I also would call. I did not trust some of the people who would come and help at the home. I called the center and asked Melvin's case worker remove and find Melvin another place. The day we were moving Melvin, the owner took an item that I knew Melvin had in his possession; my father gave it to him. When I asked about the item, the owner stated he never saw it. I knew I was doing the right thing in removing my son.

The next place the center sent me to was a breath of fresh air. It was the home of a couple that Melvin is with to this day. It was not run as a group home. It is a loving, caring environment. They have a son, and Melvin was included to their family.

Melvin would come home on the weekends. Even though he was not living with us, the tension between him and his dad was still there. Melvin wanted his dad to love him, and his dad wanted him to be who he thought he should be. His dad could not accept him as he was.

When Melvin asked to be set free, he instilled in me that same dream. I was in an abusive, controlled marriage. When I lost the election in 2000, I prayed and asked God what should I do. A friend of mine told me to try the airlines. So I went back to school. The program I enrolled in had many choices of a career in the airline industry such as ticket agent, baggage, flight attendant, and a small business career as a travel agent. I selected ticket agent; let's just say that was my plan. I could fly anywhere, and that was my getaway.

The instructor wanted me to select flight attendant.

I said, "No, I am afraid to fly."

She tried many times to change my mind, but I would not until an unexpected event.

My grandmother (my dad's mother) passed away that year. We flew from California to New Orleans. I was terrified. Every bump, shake, dip, and noise, I would cry and shake. The children's dad was angry, not sympathetic. He was saying unkind things, and one of the flight attendants overheard. She told him not to talk to her that way. Once we landed, we drove to the small town in Mississippi outside of Jackson, and it took the entire ride for me to calm down.

Saying my goodbyes to my grandmother was not easy; my dad passed away before she did. She was one hundred four years old, and as I stood at the grave site where she was buried next to my dad, I felt a breeze, and tears were falling from my eyes. I looked around, and all the others had left and went back to the church up the hill. As I stood alone in my tears, I heard someone whispering in my ear, "Bonnie, you cannot be afraid all your life; you will miss out on your blessings.

The next flight back home, I boarded the plane without fear. As I sat down, I could hear an inner voice say look around, watch how the flight attendants ease around the cabin. This is their work home environment; before takeoff, I prayed and asked God to take this fear of flying from me. When the wheels lift off the ground, I was not afraid. I was relaxed and enjoyed the flight. The spouse was wondering why I was not crying and afraid. I told him I prayed, and God took the fear away. He did not utter another word to me.

When I went back to class, I told the instructor to sign me up. I want to be a flight attendant. I told her what happened, and I was not afraid to fly anymore.

One weekend before I left for training in Houston, I told Melvin that I got a job. I was going to be a flight attendant.

Melvin told me, "Good, Momma, everybody should have a job." He also told me he wanted a house and to drive a car. My son still had his dreams for himself.

As I stated earlier, I removed my youngest daughter from the school district because of the cruelty of some of the teachers toward her because of me. Their dad was in a scandal that was printed in the paper throughout the region. She was teased not just by the kids but also by some of the teaching staff. Her oldest sister was in college and not at home. Their dad was not taking good care of our youngest daughter. I sent her to another state with relatives to finish out her school year. She was upset and hurt that she did not get to graduate with her friends, but I needed her to be safe. We have since talked about it, and I explained why, and I said I was sorry. I know that was hard on her. She is now married with two beautiful children, and I have a wonderful son-in-law whom I dearly love. I filed for divorce two years after I started flying. I am retired from flying now. God blessed me with a new loving husband.

Melvin is thriving. I am blessed that he has been with loving caretakers. His dad does not see him much, maybe every two to three years. This breaks my heart because Melvin loves his dad and longs for him to accept him and love him. He asks me all the time why his dad does not see him.

He asked, "Is my dad ever going to see me again?"

My answer to him is the same: "One day he will."

That is my hope and prayer. God loves us beyond our looks, how much money we have or do not have. God loves us without conditions. This is the way in which we are to love as God loves us.

Melvin can ski, I cannot, he can bowl, I am terrible at that. Melvin loves unconditionally. How many of us can truly love without limits? Our love is limited because we place conditions on love. When we see a person with a disability, often some show pity. Why? Some show disgust. Why? Do we all have challenges in our lives? We have become so judgmental and self-absorbed that we miss out on the outpouring of love that is provided to us through those we view as different. When a person is selfish, unloving, unforgiving, judging, rude, disrespectful, insensitive, and all the other negative adjectives, you are limited, or you too can be viewed disabled because you are unable to receive the goodness and love. So who is better off?

When I was in the desert of my life, I would cry and question God, "Why me?" I would search in my thoughts for what I had done to cause me to have a disabled child. I thought about the food I ate, did I hurt someone's feelings? I recall a little boy that lived next door to us when I was a child. He would get up early in the morning and swing all day if he could. He did not talk. He hummed. I was mean to him and poked fun of him when I was a child. I thought, this is why I was being punished; or when I was in the hospital at the age of fourteen for major surgery, I saw a child that had Down syndrome locked in a crib that was built like a cage. I went over and touched him because I had never seen a baby like that before. I later thought that was my crime?

I was searching for answers in the wrong place. My thoughts of what did I do or why me have changed. Why not me? What a privilege to have experienced having a child with a disability. What a lesson of love and being loved God taught me through my son Melvin. Yes, it was hard, but I gained more and lost nothing. God was there with me through it all. God began to set me free of my past and the deep hurts by my son being in my life.

I enjoy watching movies with a message, and every now and then, there is one that sticks out. The name of the movie is *Jack*. In this movie, the character Jack was homeschooled. The disability he had was aging. He was growing old, and he was young. As the movie goes on, Jack begin to understand that he does not have much time to live. His mind is young but his body aging. He began to give up, and the instructor tried to encourage him. He told him why he like teaching children—because it reminded him of the simple enjoyable things in life, riding a bike, splashing in water.

But Jack, feeling sorry for himself, said, "I want to be a regular kid."

The teacher told him about the stars, how wonderful they were but the special one was a shooting star.

He said again, "I just want to be a regular kid."

The teacher told him, "You will never be a regular kid, you are a spectacular kid."

That is my Melvin, unique.

I had blamed myself for so many years, feeling that Father God was punishing me. It took all these years of healing and learning that God was not punishing me, but he gave me Melvin because He knew I would love him unconditionally as the Lord loves all of us unconditionally.

God held on to me through Melvin, and I reached for God because he is my help in times of trouble. God is teaching me unselfish love. I was nineteen years old when I had Melvin, and it was not about me anymore, it was about him. God is also teaching me to forgive those who do not know how to love unconditionally.

Melvin did not have a loving village, for they shunned him, but Melvin had God and me. Melvin had what Father God instilled in him: the will to move forward.

I once dreamed that Melvin and I went for a walk, and I heard that Jesus was here. We started looking for him. When I saw him, Melvin left my side to run to Jesus, who was kneeling with his arms open wide. I awoke.

Do I hope in my heart that the loving, sleeping giant awakes? Yes, yes, I do!

John 9:1–3 (NIV)

As he went along, (Jesus) he saw a man blind from birth. His disciples asked him, "Rabbi, who sinned, this man or his parents, that he was born blind?"

"Neither this man nor his parents sinned," said Jesus, "but this happened so that the work of God might be displayed in his life."

Epilogue

My hope and prayer continue to be that Melvin's awareness will open but if my prayer is not as I may hope for. I am nonetheless, hopeful. Melvin has a loving spirit. He is loved by God, I love him, his sisters love him. He is surrounded with friends from his church family and caretakers who love him. I would not change anything if I had an opportunity. I look back and see God's footprints all around me. From the time of my challenging childhood to the challenges of living as an adult. One thing I know. I can not live my life without Jesus Christ. He is with me in all circumstances and He is teaching me to live in His peace.

I thank Him for Melvin and all my ashes in my life is a sweet savory of praises unto the Lord. **Extraordinary Ways of God**

Extraordinary Ways of God

As I reflect upon my life,
all the difficulties I went through

The pain of it escapes me
I am now at a place
that I thought I would not be

It is the extraordinary ways of God

Like the rushing of the ocean
his love lifted me and brought me to this place
it is where I should be

The power of His love
protected me
He restored me
He set my heart frec

It is the extraordinary ways of God

His spirit guides me through each day
even when i feel lonely
along the way

He instructs my heart
to keep me strong when storms come my way

It is the extraordinary ways of God

His love is the greatest story ever told
an ordinary person I am

His love captured me
He works in me and through me
His plan for me exceeds all the thoughts that
I thought I could be
He keeps me in His love and care

It is the extraordinary ways of God

poem from, Words of Praise, Joy, and Love

About the Author

Bernadette Butler is a wife and mother of three children and two step-children. Born and raised in Chicago, Illinois, her home life was challenging. Later, she moved to Southern California, where she lived for thirty years. She later made Ohio her home. Bernadette has lived an adventurous life. She went from computer data entry to; serving two terms as a school board member, State of California Legislature Woman of the year 1994, flight attendant, school crossing guard and finally, author. Her passion is writing poetry. She self-published in 2016 a collection of poems, *"Words of Praise, Joy and Love"*, expressing her relationship with God and all he has brought her through. Her desire is to share her story about her journey with her son, who has autism. Her hope is to inspire and encourage parents and the children who have the disorder.

CPSIA information can be obtained
at www.ICGtesting.com
Printed in the USA
BVHW03s2149231018
531072BV00001B/40/P

9 781641 386043